Foreword／はじめに

For the past decade, I have been trying to develop improved forms of TOEIC® L&R instruction that will better benefit students and help them achieve higher scores on the TOEIC® L&R Test. With reading, the ___ ___ or improving your score is simple: you must practice ___ ___ ding questions in this book were written with a spec ___ ___ hotels, office) in mind. This is to help students antic ___ ___ problems aimed at their English level. This should le ___ ___ motivate students to practice further. Doing this is the only way one can truly improve one's TOEIC® L&R reading ability.

Matthew Wilson

・・

TOEIC® L&R リーディングスコアアップのためには、基礎的な文法力と語彙力、そして TOEIC® L&R の形式を知り慣れることが大切です。本書はそれらの能力を総合的に高めることを目的に編集されていますので、この一冊を繰り返しやるだけでも TOEIC® L&R に求められる文法力と語彙力、そして頻出問題のシーンやパターンを知ることが可能です。問題に取り組むむときは、書かれている状況を推測しながら読み進めましょう。パート５とパート６の文法、語彙問題は繰り返し問題を解いてください。パート６の文章挿入問題とパート７は、本文の中に必ず答えを見つけるための手がかりがあるはずです。解法のためのプロセスが本書を通して見えてくるはずです。

鶴岡　公幸

・・

英語はスポーツと同じです。サッカーで勝つために、基本のドリブル練習や、実践での練習試合を重ねるのと同様に、TOEIC® L&R のリーディングスコアアップにも、「語彙力」と「文法力」の基本のルールを覚え、実際に「解く」実践トレーニングが必須です。本書では、最新の『頻出語彙問題』、『頻出文法問題』で基礎を固めながら、『出題パターンに慣れる』実践練習が可能です。また、TOEIC® L&R のリーディングセクションでは、限りある制限時間を上手に配分し、得意なテーマの問題でより得点を獲ることが鍵となります。本書は、頻出テーマに分かれているため、自分が得意なテーマ、苦手なテーマを知ることができます。学習は、自分の弱点を知ることから始まります。学習後には、復習するべき項目が明確になるはずです。本書が、多くの方の TOEIC® L&R スコアアップ、英語力向上に役立つことを願っています。

佐藤　千春

Business World

Incomplete Sentences

Select the best answer to complete the sentence. Then choose the letter (A), (B), (C), or (D).

1. You are ------- to become familiar with our corporate philosophy.

   (A) encourages   (B) encouraging   (C) encouraged   (D) encourage

2. Compared ------- New York City, hotels here are reasonable.

   (A) of   (B) out   (C) by   (D) with

3. Presenting ------- product's superiority is an effective marketing strategy.

   (A) our   (B) we   (C) ours   (D) us

4. Most of our clients are ------- about the launch of our new product.

   (A) exciting   (B) to excite   (C) excitement (D) excited

5. We don't currently ------- this item, but we have a similar type of product over here.

   (A) bring   (B) carry   (C) hold   (D) pack

6. To generate the greatest response, a questionnaire should be short and -------.

   (A) simple   (B) simply   (C) simplify   (D) simpler

7. Please look at the results of the employee survey ------- online.

   (A) checked   (B) conducted   (C) played   (D) supervised

8. This special offer is only available to customers ------- have placed orders.

   (A) whichever   (B) whose   (C) whoever   (D) who

Text Completion

Select the best answer to complete the text. Then choose the letter (A), (B), (C), or (D).

Questions 9-12 refer to the following advertisement.

Let Adventure Games plan your next employee outing or team-building activity. Deciding your company outing can be a big ------. At Adventure Games we'll do
9.
the work by listening to your needs, ------ suggesting and organizing multiple
10.
outing ideas, like go-karting, paintball, and bowling. Company outings ------ to
11.
boost teamwork, enhance workplace connections and friendships, and inspire fresh ideas. A well-planned experience can prove to be invaluable. ------.
12.

9. (A) festival   (B) trouble   (C) dispute   (D) burden

10. (A) further   (B) then   (C) besides   (D) once

11. (A) show   (B) showing   (C) are showing   (D) have been shown

12. (A) Contact us to learn more information.
    (B) Let us decide the menu for your company's special party.
    (C) Please notify us of any employee allergies or food requests.
    (D) We look forward to hearing about your adventures.

Questions 13-14 refer to the following schedule.

Sandra Wagner
Week of October 12-16

Mon. Oct. 12	8:00:	Sales meeting about new shoes
	12:00:	Lunch meeting with retailers
	2:00:	Mike Stevens' talk on in-store advertising
Tues. Oct. 13	2:00:	Discuss new outlets of ABC Shopping Mall downtown
Wed. Oct. 14		
Thurs. Oct. 15	Morning :	Meeting (New Branch Location)
Thurs. Oct. 15	Afternoon :	Supervise store's service during business hours
Fri. Oct. 16	10:00:	Meet with new recruits

13. What day is Ms. Wagner the most available?

(A) Monday

(B) Tuesday

(C) Wednesday

(D) Thursday

14. What will Ms. Wagner do on Thursday?

(A) Meet with retailers

(B) Discuss in-store advertising

(C) Observe outlet operations

(D) Meet new employees

The Big Apple Boys-New York's
Fastest Bike Messengers

Serving all five boroughs of New York—Bronx, Manhattan, Queens, Brooklyn and Staten Island—for over two decades.

Our service in a nutshell:

We deliver anything that can be safely carried in a backpack. Most of our jobs consist of the delivery of important/official documents across the Big Apple.

Basic Delivery Rates

Time		Within 2 hours	Within 1 hour	Within 30 min
Distance	0-10 blocks	$15	$25	$35
	10-30 blocks	$25	$35	$50
	30-60 blocks	$40	$50	$100

Insurance can also be applied to any parcel for $10.

Please call us at (211) 454-3220 so that we may add you to our list of satisfied customers.

15. How long has this company been in business?

(A) 5 years

(B) 10 years

(C) 15 years

(D) 20 years

16. How much would an insured delivery, 20 blocks away, within 30 minutes cost?

(A) $50

(B) $60

(C) $70

(D) $80

Education

Part 5

Incomplete Sentences

Select the best answer to complete the sentence. Then choose the letter (A), (B), (C), or (D).

1. Before ------- Japan, all international students must get a student visa.

   (A) enter   (B) entering   (C) to enter   (D) have entered

2. He ------- in psychology in university, but now he is an artist.

   (A) majored   (B) studied   (C) researched   (D) took

3. Mr. Toda helped Cathy describe ------- research plan.

   (A) hers   (B) she   (C) her   (D) herself

4. It has been 15 years since I graduated ------- university.

   (A) on   (B) in   (C) at   (D) from

5. Library accounts are automatically created, so no ------- registration is necessary.

   (A) initially   (B) initial   (C) initials   (D) initialed

6. I'm happy to have this ------- to study with such great professors.

   (A) notice   (B) benefit   (C) factor   (D) opportunity

7. Statistics is a ------- class for second-year students.

   (A) require   (B) required   (C) requiring   (D) requires

8. The geologists plan to study the soil from the mountains ------- Canberra.

   (A) out   (B) next   (C) onto   (D) around

Text Completion

Select the best answer to complete the text. Then choose the letter (A), (B), (C), or (D).

Questions 9-12 refer to the following web page.

LVU Campus Tours

The students of Las Vegas University are at the heart of the LVU experience,

------ tour our campus, meet LVU students, and have them guide you on a
   9.

campus tour. You can enjoy a candid conversation with ------ students, ask
                                                10.

them about classes, housing, Las Vegas, online student support, and more.

------. Doing this will hopefully give you the best idea of what LVU life would
   11.

be like for you. The two-hour campus tour allows you to experience firsthand

everything you need to know. Click here for ------ your guided tour.
                                          12.

---

9. (A) so   (B) then   (C) also   (D) and

10. (A) now   (B) modern   (C) latest   (D) current

11. (A) We will match you with a guide based on your interests and goals.
    (B) Feel free to ask about other universities found in the area.
    (C) Take the time to learn more about the city of Las Vegas online.
    (D) Please let us know the kind of person you were in high school.

12. (A) arrange
    (B) to arrange
    (C) arranging
    (D) arrangement

Reading Comprehension

Select the best answer for each question and mark the letter (A), (B), (C), or (D).

Questions 13-14 refer to the following notice.

University of Colorado

• **Undergraduate Programs**

All required supporting documents* must be received by the following deadlines.

Fall: May 31, Spring: Sep. 30, Summer: Feb. 28

• **Intensive English Program**

The Intensive English Program has two additional deadlines:

July 31 for the Fall session (beginning in October)

December 31 for the Spring session (beginning in March)

*application fee, transcripts, GPA requirements, English proficiency scores, financial documents, passport copy, letter of recommendation

---

13. Who is this notice intended for?

(A) High school students in Colorado

(B) International students

(C) Both domestic and international students

(D) University of Colorado program transfer students

14. When is the due date for students interested in the program from March?

(A) February 28

(B) May 31

(C) July 31

(D) December 31

Questions 15-16 refer to the following report.

A poll of university students found some interesting opinions about adulthood and maturity. Considering most young people start college at age 18 or 19, the average age most expected to find a full-time job is 21.4. This means a lot of them take about three years to find a full-time job after high school graduation or that students are skipping graduation and getting almost a year's head start in the job market.

Goal in life	Average age expected to achieve this goal
First full-time job	21.4
College graduation	22.4
Marriage	27.5
Birth of first child	28.3

15. According to the report, when do students think they will finish school?

   (A) At 21.4 years of age
   (B) At 22.4 years of age
   (C) At 27.5 years of age
   (D) At 28.3 years of age

16. According to the report, how soon after college do students expect to be married?

   (A) About 3 years after
   (B) About 4 years after
   (C) About 5 years after
   (D) About 6 years after

Daily Life

Part 5
Incomplete Sentences

Select the best answer to complete the sentence. Then choose the letter (A), (B), (C), or (D).

1. All participants have to arrive ten minutes before ------- scheduled appointments.

   (A) they   (B) their   (C) them   (D) themselves

2. At the book reading workshop, authors read books ------- to children.

   (A) fully   (B) aloud   (C) noisy   (D) over

3. We are pleased to ------- a new exchange student from Canada.

   (A) welcoming   (B) welcome   (C) welcomed   (D) welcomes

4. Use this robot vacuum cleaner after reading the ------- carefully.

   (A) systems   (B) policies   (C) applications (D) directions

5. The order can ------- anywhere in the world.

   (A) ships   (B) to ship   (C) be shipping   (D) be shipped

6. Steven began a bakery more than 20 years -------.

   (A) last   (B) ago   (C) past   (D) before

7. The air conditioner we bought was designed to turn off -------.

   (A) automatic   (B) automatically (C) automated   (D) automate

8. The Momo Store also has small items you can ------- as souvenirs.

   (A) replace   (B) borrow   (C) purchase   (D) sell

Text Completion

Select the best answer to complete the text. Then choose the letter (A), (B), (C), or (D).

Questions 9-12 refer to the following notice.

Security Notice by Artist Request

The use of cellphones, cameras, smart watches or recording devices will not be permitted during tonight's performance. Guests are encouraged to leave these items in their home or vehicle ------ to entry. Failure to comply with this
9.
policy will result in ------ from the venue without a refund. We greatly ------ your
10.   11.
cooperation in creating a phone-free viewing experience. ------.
12.

Thank you for your understanding.

Central Theater

---

9. (A) once   (B) when   (C) advance   (D) prior

10. (A) remove   (B) removing   (C) removal   (D) removed

11. (A) anticipate   (B) acknowledge   (C) acquire   (D) appreciate

12. (A) Further details about this policy can be found on our website.
    (B) Come celebrate our 25th anniversary this Saturday from 5:00 P.M.
    (C) For information on group rates and private events, check online.
    (D) Check for details to see if you qualify for exclusion to this rule.

Part 7

Reading Comprehension

Select the best answer for each question and mark the letter (A), (B), (C), or (D).

Questions 13-14 refer to the following invitation.

Happy 30th!!

Join us as we celebrate Lucy's special day!

London Bar & Grill
1203 Chestnut Ave.

Saturday, August 5
Dinner & desserts 7:00-8:30 p.m.
Birthday cake at 8:00
Live music and dance for the older crowd 9:00 ~

RSVP to Miranda Williams by
July 20
mwilliams@zmail.com

13. What is the purpose of this invitation?

(A) To notify of a party

(B) To ask for monetary support

(C) To participate in a music concert

(D) To give directions to the venue

14. What should interested people do?

(A) Contact Lucy

(B) Inform Ms. Williams

(C) Call the venue

(D) Come without notice

Questions 15-16 refer to the following report.

Napa Valley Weather Forecast

5-Day Weather Forecast

Today:	Lots of sunshine. High 90F
Tonight:	Mostly clear. Low 55F
Tomorrow:	Partly cloudy. High 78F and low of 56F
Sunday:	Afternoon showers and thunderstorms likely. Highs in the low 80s and lows in the low 60s.
Monday:	Cloudy. High in the low 70s and lows in the mid 50s.
Tuesday:	Partly cloudy. High in the mid 70s and lows in the low 50s.

15. Which day will be the coldest?

    (A) Saturday

    (B) Sunday

    (C) Monday

    (D) Tuesday

16. According to the forecast, which statement is true?

    (A) Rain is expected Sunday afternoon.

    (B) The weather will be consistent all week.

    (C) The weather is expected to be severe.

    (D) Saturday will have the sunniest weather.

Health

Part 5

Incomplete Sentences

Select the best answer to complete the sentence. Then choose the letter (A), (B), (C), or (D).

1. My health check result ------- states that I need to go on a diet immediately.

   (A) clear   (B) clearly   (C) clearer   (D) cleared

2. People should exercise regularly ------- a daily basis.

   (A) by   (B) from   (C) on   (D) to

3. The receptionist asked each patient to present ------- insurance card.

   (A) they   (B) them   (C) their   (D) themselves

4. Doctors need to ------- understand patients' health conditions.

   (A) openly   (B) quickly   (C) certainly   (D) truly

5. Do not stop ------- this medicine unless instructed by a doctor.

   (A) take   (B) took   (C) taking   (D) taken

6. Many doctors will ------- introduce consultations over the Internet.

   (A) yet   (B) since   (C) ever   (D) soon

7. The USS Hospital ------- cutting-edge healthcare in fields such as cancer treatment.

   (A) provide   (B) providing   (C) to provide   (D) provides

8. You can get your medicine from the pharmacy ------- from the hospital.

   (A) inside   (B) along   (C) across   (D) through

Text Completion

Select the best answer to complete the text. Then choose the letter (A), (B), (C), or (D).

Questions 9-12 refer to the following internal memo.

Dear colleagues,

As you know, the annual health check will take place next Tuesday and Friday mornings. I feel I must ------ you that these examinations are not optional. You
   9.
have an obligation to ------ these health exams in order to use our company's
   10.
health insurance plan. There are no other scheduled health check dates for this

year. ------. Opting out of these times may be unavoidable. If that's the case,
   11.
you are required to organize a doctor's visit on your own. You will be reimbursed

for this expense, but all ------ will need to be submitted to Accounting.
   12.

Feel free to discuss these details with your supervisor.

Thank you,

Drake Barron

CEO, Crazy Games, Inc.

9. (A) remind   (B) reminder   (C) reminding   (D) to remind

10. (A) contact   (B) practice   (C) challenge   (D) undergo

11. (A) I realize these times may not be compatible with your schedule.
    (B) Any objections to this policy should be told to management.
    (C) Health insurance rates can be negotiated in person.
    (D) The visiting doctors and health professionals are the top in their field.

12. (A) money   (B) receipts   (C) notifications   (D) invoices

Reading Comprehension

Select the best answer for each question and mark the letter (A), (B), (C), or (D).

Questions 13-14 refer to the following article.

According to a report entitled, "2020 Health Outlook", an average adult laughs only about 12 times per day, while an average child laughs about 120 times a day. The report has shown that laughter can be a form of stomach exercise for your internal organs improving the blood flow in your veins, as well as releasing hormones in your brain that are good for your immune system. Possibly the most interesting finding of the studies was that faking laughter had the same positive effect on the body even if the laughter was not real. So just pretending to laugh can be good for you as well. It seems that even science has now admitted that laughter is the best medicine.

13. According to the article, what effect does laughter have?

(A) It weakens one's immune system.

(B) It regulates blood pressure.

(C) It builds a sense of humor.

(D) It improves blood flow.

14. What effect does fake laughter have on the body?

(A) It's the same as real laughter.

(B) It's worse than real laughter.

(C) It's better than real laughter.

(D) It's not well known.

TO: mikeb@qualitymill.com
FROM: nancy@global.com

Mike,

Thank you for your advice on losing weight. I have started exercising and cutting down on fried food and sweets. Last week, I went without meat and ice cream for three days! Also, I started doing floor exercises and then jogging for about one mile every day.

Drinking lots of water also helped me cut down on eating lots of food, just like you said.

Again, thank you for all your advice.

Best wishes,
Nancy

15. **What kind of advice did Nancy NOT get from Mike?**

(A) To reduce fried food meals

(B) To wear warmer clothes

(C) To drink lots of water

(D) To do floor exercises

16. **What did Mike do for Nancy?**

(A) He gave her some food and sweets.

(B) He gave some tips to lose weight.

(C) He jogged with her for hours.

(D) He supervised floor exercises.

Scene **5**

Job Interviews

Part 5

Incomplete Sentences

Select the best answer to complete the sentence. Then choose the letter (A), (B), (C), or (D).

1. All ------- should send us a resume including one reference letter.
   (A) appliers   (B) applications   (C) applicants   (D) applying

2. We attached a detailed job ------- to this letter.
   (A) description   (B) subject   (C) matter   (D) substance

3. I'm writing to you about the job ------- in your department.
   (A) open   (B) to open   (C) opened   (D) opening

4. I encouraged him to think about the management -------.
   (A) part   (B) duty   (C) position   (D) role

5. We received your ------- registration form today.
   (A) completion   (B) completed   (C) completely   (D) completing

6. He has a Master of Science degree and has been working ------- the past three years.
   (A) for   (B) in   (C) since   (D) at

7. You need to submit the ------- to confirm you finished the minimum of ten days of training.
   (A) certify   (B) certificated   (C) certificate   (D) certified

8. We're looking for someone ------- in the IT industry.
   (A) evaluated   (B) challenging   (C) outgoing   (D) experienced

Text Completion

Select the best answer to complete the text. Then choose the letter (A), (B), (C), or (D).

Questions 9-12 refer to the following e-mail.

From: alansandler@blackbananadesign.com

To: jeffbland@geemail.com

Date: Monday, July 6

Subject: Invitation to Interview

Dear Jeff Bland,

Thank you for applying for the position of office administrator with Black Banana Design. We would like to invite you to come for an interview ------ **9.** scheduled for July 13, at 1 P.M. Let us know at your ------ **10.** convenience if this time does not suit you and we will reschedule things.

At our office, you will have to obtain a visitor's pass from security in the lobby, at which time you may be asked to show ------ **11.** identification.

For the interview, bring in your portfolio. ------. **12.** You do not need to bring in extra copies of anything.

Contact me if you have any questions about the interview process.

Sincerely,

Alan Sandler

Art Director

Black Banana Design

---

9. (A) definitely   (B) tentatively   (C) surely   (D) certainly

10. (A) early   (B) earlier   (C) earliest   (D) earliness

11. (A) a few   (B) a little   (C) much   (D) some

12. (A) Please be prepared to talk about your designs in detail.
    (B) If we like them, we will ask you to come in for an interview.
    (C) We will pay you for any of the designs that we use.
    (D) Congratulations and I look forward to working with you.

Reading Comprehension

Select the best answer for each question and mark the letter (A), (B), (C), or (D).

Questions 13-14 refer to the following memo.

To: All TBQ personnel
From: Chris Johnson, General Manager

February's crew evaluations of The Burger Queen staff are finished. Again, we use these bi-annual assessments to reward those who did well with promotions and raises. Crew are evaluated on work attendance, customer comments, and on my personal observations of your performance at work.

If you don't receive a pay raise this time, yet you feel you deserve one, please come and discuss these concerns with me before or after your shift. Remember that the next evaluation will be in six months.

Chris Johnson
General Manager
The Burger Queen

13. What is NOT an area of evaluation by management?

    (A) Workplace attendance

    (B) Starting work early

    (C) Customer feedback

    (D) Management observations

14. What is suggested from this memo?

    (A) All staff will be rewarded.

    (B) Some staff will lose their jobs.

    (C) All staff will lose their jobs.

    (D) Some staff will be rewarded.

Questions 15-16 refer to the following text-message chain.

Kate Chang	13:08

Hello, Kate Chang here. I have an interview with your advertising department at 2:00 today. I tried calling but couldn't get through.

Timothy Wilson	13:20

Hi, Kate. Yes, we're expecting you at 2:00. Is everything OK?

Kate Chang	13:22

Well, no. I'm stuck in some bad traffic. I'm afraid I won't make it. Is there anything that can be done?

Timothy Wilson	13:23

OK, we can meet you later. How about 4:00 instead?

Kate Chang	13:25

Sorry. That won't work. I have another appointment at 4:00. Can I reschedule the interview for the same time tomorrow or later this week?

Timothy Wilson	13:26

No problem, Kate. How about tomorrow? Same time.

Kate Chang	13:28

Perfect. Apologies. I'll plan on an alternative route tomorrow.

15. Who most likely is Kate Chang?

(A) A taxi driver

(B) A job applicant

(C) A university student

(D) A marketing manager

16. At 13:22, what does Kate Chang mean when she writes, "I'm afraid I won't make it"?

(A) She'll change her means of transportation.

(B) She's refusing to submit her resume.

(C) She cannot keep her appointment.

(D) She's decided to try a different route.

Meetings

Part 5

Incomplete Sentences

Select the best answer to complete the sentence. Then choose the letter (A), (B), (C), or (D).

1. Ms. Sarisati urged newcomers to share ------- opinions.

   (A) they   (B) theirs   (C) their   (D) them

2. Henry was strongly opposed ------- the introduction of the new system.

   (A) for   (B) to   (C) among   (D) against

3. This result helps us ------- what consumers will want over the next few years.

   (A) determining   (B) determined   (C) determination   (D) determine

4. Please reply to this e-mail only ------- you cannot attend.

   (A) that   (B) yet   (C) also   (D) if

5. The new budget request ------- by the board of directors.

   (A) approves   (B) was approving   (C) was approved   (D) approved

6. We have to take the ------- of the meeting and e-mail them to everyone later.

   (A) minutes   (B) notes   (C) memorandums   (D) items

7. At the annual shareholders meeting yesterday, his retirement was ------- announced.

   (A) formal   (B) formalism   (C) formality   (D) formally

8. The new department meeting will be held ------- Wednesday starting in May.

   (A) every   (B) from   (C) enough   (D) since

Text Completion

Select the best answer to complete the text. Then choose the letter (A), (B), (C), or (D).

Questions 9-12 refer to the following e-mail.

Hello everyone,

I hope your weekend was nice and relaxing.

Regarding tomorrow's monthly meeting: regrettably we have to ------- it to
9.
another date later this month. My ------- to you for this sudden notice.
10.

Due to unforeseen circumstances, Shelly Winter cannot be with us this week.
Without her, we can't really discuss a lot of the issues on the meeting's -------,
11.
so upper management advised me to reschedule things.

In the meantime, those of you who haven't completed the online job satisfaction
survey yet, please do so. -------.
12.

The date of the next meeting will be decided later this week, at which point I will
e-mail you again with the new date and time.

Thank you,

Dave Santos

---

9. (A) cancel   (B) remove   (C) later   (D) postpone

10. (A) apologizing   (B) apologies   (C) apologize   (D) apologized

11. (A) bulletin   (B) list   (C) agenda   (D) index

12. (A) These results will be the focus of our next meeting.
     (B) If you are unhappy at your job, please talk to Human Resources.
     (C) Let us know which meeting day is better for you.
     (D) Talk to me if you have things you want to tell Shelly.

Select the best answer for each question and mark the letter (A), (B), (C), or (D).

Questions 13-14 refer to the following letter.

Hey Matt,

It's me, Tom White. We met briefly at the reception party at the conference. There were a lot of people there last night, so I hope you remember me.

It sounded like you were interested in some of the online workshops we offer.

If it's no problem, I'd like to organize a meeting sometime this week to see what we can do.

Let me know when you're available.

Sincerely,

Tom White

13. What is the purpose of this letter?

    (A) To apply for a job opening

    (B) To schedule an appointment

    (C) To offer discounted products

    (D) To suggest canceling a meeting

14. When did Mr. White meet Matt?

    (A) The day before yesterday

    (B) Yesterday

    (C) Early this morning

    (D) Around noon today

Questions 15-16 refer to the following agenda.

Agenda

· Introductory remarks by President, Mike Takeda

· HR Manager, David Graham, a briefing on the new online training program

· Discussion of the above by HR Director, Crista Green

· Assistant HR Manager, Kevin Thomas, possible future system modifications

· Discussion of any other related issues

---

15. **What is one feature of the company's training course?**
    (A) It will be online.
    (B) It will be an outdoor retreat.
    (C) It will be a workshop.
    (D) It will be through video conferencing.

16. **Who mostly likely is in charge of improving the future system?**
    (A) Mike Takeda
    (B) David Graham
    (C) Crista Green
    (D) Kevin Thomas

Money

Part 5

Incomplete Sentences

Select the best answer to complete the sentence. Then choose the letter (A), (B), (C), or (D).

1. Accountants help clients ------- decisions about their investments.

   (A) make   (B) making   (C) made   (D) makes

2. It is recommended to get travel insurance ------- any overseas trips.

   (A) except   (B) before   (C) of   (D) until

3. Please login to your account to ------- your contact information within 24 hours.

   (A) verify   (B) verified   (C) verification   (D) verifying

4. The staff responded that the project was still kept ------- the budget.

   (A) till   (B) within   (C) instead   (D) despite

5. The ------- rate on this credit card is about 18%.

   (A) interesting   (B) interested   (C) interest   (D) interests

6. My principle is to ------- borrow nor lend money.

   (A) both   (B) but   (C) either   (D) neither

7. The accounting report will be discussed ------- than planned in the meeting.

   (A) latest   (B) late   (C) later   (D) lately

8. Ron told me he can't ------- to buy a new computer at present.

   (A) afford   (B) pay   (C) take   (D) have

Text Completion

Select the best answer to complete the text. Then choose the letter (A), (B), (C), or (D).

Questions 9-12 refer to the following website.

Cash Money to Electronic Money

Electronic money, or better known as e-money, is the modern form of money in which all transactions are made electronically. The idea of e-money is still young but its ------ for use in various transactions has made it a big hit.
9.
Today it ------ in every part of world. ------, e-money works similar to paper
10. **11.**
money without the risks and inconvenience which may occur with cash money. The use of the Internet gave a great boost to the use of the computer for monetary transactions. ------. This fact is enough to prove the increasing
12.
popularity of e-money over cash money.

---

9. (A) reliability   (B) discovery   (C) prosperity   (D) probability

10. (A) uses   (B) used   (C) is using   (D) is being used

11. (A) Absolutely   (B) Basically   (C) Really   (D) Barely

12. (A) People still prefer to use cash when buying items like food, though.
     (B) Today, 90% of transactions are done through online payment systems.
     (C) The popularity of the Internet has made newspapers outdated.
     (D) There may be a day when e-money will be more popular than cash money.

Reading Comprehension

Select the best answer for each question and mark the letter (A), (B), (C), or (D).

Questions 13-14 refer to the following table.

Financial Report for Mad Club Restaurant Group

	1st Quarter	2nd Quarter	3rd Quarter	4th Quarter
Sales	$545,234	$456,009	$609,090	$750,980
Net Income	$65,230	$46,090	$34,900	$67,810
Net Income per share	$4.68	$3.67	$4.23	$5.70

13. Which quarter showed the largest amount of company profit?

   (A) 1st quarter

   (B) 2nd quarter

   (C) 3rd quarter

   (D) 4th quarter

14. What is the sales trend the last three quarters?

   (A) Stable

   (B) Increasing

   (C) Unstable

   (D) Decreasing

Questions 15-16 refer to the following webpage.

 **Panda Pay**

To use Panda Pay, you need to first verify your identity.

From the main menu, tap identity verification and choose one of the verification methods listed below.

· Bank account verification
· Verify your identity by linking your bank account to Panda Pay. See **HELP** for details.
· Verify your identity online

Use any of the acceptable forms of ID (passport, driver's license, or social security number) and follow the on-screen instructions to verify your identity.

15. What is the nature of Panda Pay?

(A) Credit card
(B) Online membership card
(C) Electronic payment system
(D) Discount card system

16. What is NOT mentioned as an acceptable form of ID?

(A) Passport
(B) Credit card
(C) Driver's license
(D) Social security number

Office Life

Incomplete Sentences

Select the best answer to complete the sentence. Then choose the letter (A), (B), (C), or (D).

1. The new copier is ------- at making copies than other leading models.

   (A) fastest   (B) fasted   (C) faster   (D) fasting

2. The boss recommended I transfer ------- the overseas branch.

   (A) at   (B) for   (C) to   (D) in

3. Mr. Sakai always responds to questions from subordinates -------.

   (A) his own   (B) he   (C) his   (D) himself

4. ------- free to contact us if you have any questions.

   (A) Be   (B) Make   (C) Come   (D) Feel

5. Return the document to the manager's office with this ------- envelope.

   (A) enclosed   (B) enclosing   (C) enclose   (D) enclosure

6. He can work well in any situation ------- he's very adaptable.

   (A) so   (B) because   (C) but   (D) while

7. Staff will be trained ------- with the new software to ensure everyone understands it.

   (A) independence   (B) independently   (C) independency   (D) independent

8. The managers' meeting will begin at 11:00 A.M. ------- 2:00 P.M.

   (A) in place of   (B) with regard to   (C) instead of   (D) in exchange for

Part 6

Text Completion

Select the best answer to complete the text. Then choose the letter (A), (B), (C), or (D).

Questions 9-12 refer to the following e-mail.

From: fredmercury@onedesign.com

To: staff@onedesign.com

Date: Friday, February 5

Subject: Weekend Floor Cleaning

Hello everyone,

It's that time of year again: the ------- floor cleaning will be this weekend. It will
                                      9.

take place all day tomorrow ------ people wanting to come in to work on the
                              10.

weekend will have to do so on Sunday. I have been told to tell you that the

cleaning staff would ------ it if you could put your chairs and any other objects
                       11.

like garbage cans on your desks and tables. ------.
                                              12.

Thank you and have a good weekend.

Fred Mercury

9. (A) average   (B) academic   (C) annual   (D) accurate

10. (A) so   (B) as   (C) by   (D) but

11. (A) appreciated   (B) appreciating   (C) appreciation   (D) appreciate

12. (A) Don't hesitate to let me know if you have any questions.
    (B) Don't forget to clean everything well.
    (C) I'm looking forward to seeing you all tomorrow.
    (D) I think it will be a good chance to get to know each other.

Select the best answer for each question and mark the letter (A), (B), (C), or (D).

Questions 13-14 refer to the following memo.

TO: All Hotel Managers
RE: Overtime

We are seeking to keep costs down for the coming busy Christmas season, so all hotel managers are requested to target overtime to less than 50 hours per week total. Needless to say, overtime is costly to our bottom line and last Christmas season our overtime expenditures exceeded our budget targets. If overtime hours totals exceed 50 hours for your hotel, contact each personnel representative immediately and new staff will be assigned to you to ease the overtime workload.

Thanks,

Drew
Personnel Manager

---

13. What is the purpose of this memo?
   (A) To recruit new managers
   (B) To provide better customer service
   (C) To thank managers for their hard work
   (D) To keep overtime costs down

14. What might be Drew's responsibility?
   (A) Accounting
   (B) Marketing
   (C) Human Resources
   (D) Information Technology

Questions 15-16 refer to the following notice.

Special Announcement

For any staff interested in listening to world-famous motivational speaker Daniel White, author of such best-sellers as *Build Your Career* and *Wake Up Your Talent*, he will be coming to do a special talk here at Coconut Food, Inc. The details of the talk are as follows:

Date: November 3

Time: 15:00-17:00

Location: Conference Room A, second floor of Main Building

Topic: Maximizing Your Potential

Capacity is limited to 120 so sign up ASAP to assure yourself a place at this exciting event.

*Coffee and snacks will be served from 16:30 during the Q&A session.

15. Who is Mr. Daniel White?

(A) The company president

(B) A guest speaker

(C) The chief researcher

(D) A university professor

16. When can the audience ask Mr. White questions?

(A) At the beginning of the seminar

(B) During the break at 16:00

(C) The last half-hour of the seminar

(D) Anytime during the seminar

Scene **9**

Recreation

Incomplete Sentences

Select the best answer to complete the sentence. Then choose the letter (A), (B), (C), or (D).

1. Her performance ------- a good impression on the audience.

   (A) made   (B) gave   (C) found   (D) served

2. The entire audience ------- the violinist loudly.

   (A) enjoyed   (B) played   (C) applauded   (D) clapped

3. Sandy Baker is one of the most ------- and successful photographers around.

   (A) skill   (B) skilled   (C) skills   (D) skillfulness

4. That ------- is famous for his modern buildings.

   (A) plumber   (B) gardener   (C) inventor   (D) architect

5. I feel like ------- out with my friend this week.

   (A) hang   (B) to hang   (C) hanging   (D) hangs

6. The exhibition of her paintings will run ------- the end of the month.

   (A) at   (B) around   (C) until   (D) before

7. He has been an ------- football fan for a long time.

   (A) enthusiast   (B) enthusiasm   (C) enthusiastically   (D) enthusiastic

8. ------- it was raining, Ms. Bai went out with her friend.

   (A) Although   (B) If   (C) However   (D) Owing to

Part 6

Text Completion

Select the best answer to complete the text. Then choose the letter (A), (B), (C), or (D).

Questions 9-12 refer to the following web page.

At Adonis Gym, we believe in the power of fitness to improve lives. We also know exercise is hard work and everyone can use a little more ------. So we've
9.
------ fitness and entertainment so that we can make serious exercise fun. Our
10.
gyms are filled with the best equipment in the ------; everything you need for a
11.
great workout. Our world-class personal trainers work with you to experience all the awesomeness that Adonis Gym has to offer at an incredibly low price.

------.
12.

9. (A) force   (B) motivation   (C) intensity   (D) opportunity

10. (A) combine   (B) combining   (C) combined   (D) combination

11. (A) industry   (B) management   (C) company   (D) commerce

12. (A) Create an online order form immediately.
    (B) Call our office to make a cancellation request.
    (C) Cheap exercise equipment available year-round.
    (D) Come into one of our locations for more details.

Reading Comprehension

Select the best answer for each question and mark the letter (A), (B), (C), or (D).

Questions 13-14 refer to the following information.

Campus Mall Theater

1850 Chestnut Avenue

Showtimes

Love Struck 2	16:00	18:30	21:00	
The Tea Ceremony	12:00	15:00	18:00	21:00
Man v. Gun	13:00	16:00	19:00	22:00
Funny Bone	10:00	13:00	15:00	

Admission:

Adults $7.50, Students $4.50, Children 12 and under $3.00, Seniors $4.50

All morning showings are 50% off regular admission price.

The Campus Mall Theater does not allow the accompaniment of pets into the building.

---

13. What is the total cost for an adult and two small children to see the earliest showing of *Funny Bone?*
    (A) $6.25
    (B) $6.75
    (C) $12.50
    (D) $13.50

14. Who would NOT be allowed to enter this theater?
    (A) An adult with many children
    (B) An elderly person with a child
    (C) A man with a dog
    (D) Children under the age of 12

Questions 15-16 refer to the following letter.

Dear Subscriber,

We thank you for your subscription order for *Cinema Life Magazine*, the most exciting magazine in movies. We would like to remind you that your subscription payment is two weeks overdue. If you would like to continue receiving issues, please send your payment no later than January 14.

If you have already sent in your payment, please disregard this letter and we thank you in advance. If you have any questions, please contact us at 1-800-998-1243.

Thank you so much.

Cinema Life Magazine

15. **What is this letter about?**

(A) An invitation to a new movie

(B) A reminder of late payment

(C) A special offer for subscribers

(D) A letter of apology

16. **What should the person do to continue receiving more magazine issues?**

(A) Call the phone number

(B) Reply to the letter

(C) Pay by the deadline

(D) Submit the subscription order

Restaurants

Part 5

Incomplete Sentences

Select the best answer to complete the sentence. Then choose the letter (A), (B), (C), or (D).

1. There are a lot of travelers ------- want to keep their food budget low.
   (A) where   (B) which   (C) who   (D) what

2. This dish contains fresh tomatoes ------- this morning.
   (A) combined   (B) removed   (C) treated   (D) harvested

3. Today's special is chicken that ------- with potatoes.
   (A) broiled   (B) has been broiling   (C) has been broiled   (D) is broiling

4. Our chef works ------- with local producers to create delicious meals.
   (A) hardly   (B) nearly   (C) closely   (D) relatively

5. We try to serve ------- baked bread every morning.
   (A) freshly   (B) fresh   (C) fresher   (D) freshness

6. At that winery, you can try a ------- variety of regional wines.
   (A) big   (B) many   (C) wide   (D) long

7. In most restaurants in Asia, you're supposed to take your bill to the -------.
   (A) drawer   (B) bank   (C) cashier   (D) registration

8. The Cowboy Bistro offers great deals on menu items ------- the week.
   (A) after   (B) toward   (C) around   (D) throughout

Part 6

Text Completion

Select the best answer to complete the text. Then choose the letter (A), (B), (C), or (D).

Questions 9-12 refer to the following web page.

The ACE Restaurant Group is a ------ player in the UK casual dining market with
 9.
over 650 restaurants and pubs all over the UK. We have a wide portfolio of well-

known brands, with Wagamama, Frankie & Black's, and Sonny Salsa's ------ our
 10.
principal restaurants. ------, Wagamama now has five locations in the US with
 11.
more to come. Our diverse portfolio of brands provides something for everyone,

and we love the variety that comes from working with all of them. ------.
 12.

9. (A) remote   (B) minimal   (C) cheap   (D) leading

10. (A) is   (B) be   (C) being   (D) to be

11. (A) In conclusion (B) To sum up (C) Of course   (D) In addition

12. (A) To make a reservation, please call this number.
    (B) For further information, feel free to contact us.
    (C) Talk to your nearest Wagamama manager for more information.
    (D) For birthdays, we recommend calling in advance.

Reading Comprehension

Select the best answer for each question and mark the letter (A), (B), (C), or (D).

Questions 13-14 refer to the following order form.

Namaste International Hotel
New DELHI
EGGS TO ORDER

Date:

Time:

TWO FARM-FRESH EGGS

☐ FRIED ☐ SCRAMBLED ☐ POACHED ☐ BOILED

Served with

☐ BACON HAM ☐ CHICKEN SAUSAGE

☐ GRILLED TOMATOES ☐ HASH BROWNS

FLUFFY THREE-EGG OMELETTE

☐ Cheese ☐ Mushroom ☐ Ham

☐ Spanish Onions ☐ Tomatoes

Special Instructions:

Name:

Table No.:

ROOM NUMBER:

13. How many kinds of egg dishes can a guest order?

(A) 1

(B) 2

(C) 3

(D) 4 or more

14. What information is NOT required for this order form?

(A) Name

(B) Phone number

(C) Table number

(D) Room number

Questions 15-16 refer to the following business card.

CHIHARU Japanese Restaurant

Level One, Thousand Springs Hotel
New Delhi, 29 Ashoka Road
Connaught Place
New Delhi-10323 India

Tel: 91 11 419340604 Ex: 1008
Fax: 91 11 419308207
chiharu-spring@thousand.com
www.chiharu-thousand.com

15. **Which floor is this restaurant located on?**

(A) The ground floor

(B) The second floor

(C) The basement

(D) The 29th floor

16. **What information is missing in this business card?**

(A) Phone number

(B) Fax number

(C) E-mail address

(D) Social media account

Cooking

Incomplete Sentences

Select the best answer to complete the sentence. Then choose the letter (A), (B), (C), or (D).

1. Taste it and adjust the ------- as you see fit.

   (A) seasoning   (B) season   (C) seasons   (D) seasoned

2. The aroma of the grilled fish stimulated my -------.

   (A) taste   (B) appetite   (C) stomach   (D) dish

3. We can start ------- day with fluffy and delicious waffles.

   (A) ours   (B) our   (C) us   (D) we

4. In order not to burn it, reduce the ------- and keep stirring.

   (A) pot   (B) temperature   (C) heat   (D) hot

5. When the chicken is cooked, add the ------- tomatoes.

   (A) chopped   (B) chopping   (C) chop   (D) to chop

6. Lightly steaming broccoli ------- more nutrients than boiling.

   (A) costs   (B) cooks   (C) gets   (D) retains

7. Microwaves are surprisingly good at ------- delicate meat.

   (A) cook   (B) cooking   (C) cooked   (D) cooks

8. Italiano Cooking Studio is a place ------- people come to learn to cook pasta and bake bread.

   (A) where   (B) what   (C) which   (D) when

Text Completion

Select the best answer to complete the text. Then choose the letter (A), (B), (C), or (D).

Questions 9-12 refer to the following advertisement.

TOP SHELF COOKING SCHOOL

Interested in becoming a better cook? Want to surprise friends and family with your newfound cooking skills? Need to use ingredients in your fridge that you'd ------ just throw away?
9.

Top Shelf Cooking School is starting a 4-week adult course for those ------
10.
answered "yes" to any of the above questions.

The new course ------ in the evenings, from 6:30 to 8:00, Monday to Thursday.
11.
Each night, we'll look at making a different dish from scratch. At the end of the evening, students will take home a photo of their meal and a recipe card of that particular dish. ------. This time together is usually the most enjoyable part of
12.
the class.

Check out our website, topshelfcooking.com, for more details. But hurry, these courses fill up fast!

---

9. (A) after all   (B) anyway   (C) nevertheless   (D) otherwise

10. (A) what   (B) who   (C) whom   (D) which

11. (A) offered   (B) is offering   (C) is offered   (D) will be offered

12. (A) Order whatever you'd like from our menu to take home with you.
     (B) If you're interested in being an instructor, e-mail us for more info.
     (C) Then, they'll be able to eat their creations with other students.
     (D) Please inquire about the various courses we have available.

Reading Comprehension

Select the best answer for each question and mark the letter (A), (B), (C), or (D).

Questions 13-17 refer to the following menu and e-mail.

Mexico Grill
Take-Out Menu

Ask about our catering options

Appetizers

Nacho Chips and Dip $8.95

Quesadillas $9.95

Mexican Spring Rolls $9.95

Soup

Black Bean Soup $7.75

Vegetable Soup $6.95

Main Course

Burritos (bean/beef/chicken) $15.95

Soft Tacos (beef/chicken/steak) $15.95

Fajitas (beef/chicken/steak) $16.95

(above items have half and half options for take-out)

Mexican Pizza $12.95
(chorizo, onion, salsa)

Mexican Steak $19.95
(with spicy baked potato)

* *one-week notice required for catering orders.*

** *there is a $50 deposit for use of stainless-steel containers for catering orders.*

*** *availability of menu items for catering is subject to change. Inquire for more information.*

 (416)-555-1234

From: simonlittle@centralhospital.com

To: maryleesanders@centralhospital.com

Date: September 13

Subject: Party Preparations

Hi Mary Lee,

Thanks for organizing last month's office party. It was great. The party you planned for July was also fun. I don't know how you find the time to plan everything as your department is so busy.

Anyway, I'm contacting you because I heard that for this month's party you're thinking of contacting the Mexican restaurant across the street. I looked at their take-out/catering menu yesterday and it would appear that most of the items are meat dishes. This might be a problem for those of us who don't eat meat or would like some other healthier choices.

Perhaps we can contact another restaurant to provide some vegetarian dishes as well. I'm not sure about the budget for these parties, so let me know if it is possible to have two locations cater or not.

In the future, if you'd like to have someone else bear the burden of planning the monthly office parties, then I would be more than happy to take over. Again, you are doing a great job and I think everyone appreciates it.

Sincerely,

Simon Little

13. **What should people who want catering do?**
    - (A) Order each item on the menu
    - (B) Pay to use special containers
    - (C) Order one day before event
    - (D) Pay everything in advance

14. **What can people ordering take-out do?**
    - (A) Sample food
    - (B) Pay with a credit card
    - (C) Mix main dish ingredients
    - (D) Order online

15. **What is the main purpose of the e-mail?**
    - (A) To point out a problem with the menu
    - (B) To express appreciation for everything
    - (C) To decline an invitation
    - (D) To recommend a successor

16. **What does Simon Little suggest?**
    - (A) Canceling the monthly event
    - (B) Adding more food options
    - (C) Having someone else plan it
    - (D) Increasing the budget

17. **What does the e-mail suggest about Mary Lee?**
    - (A) She works at a restaurant.
    - (B) She often organizes office events.
    - (C) She works in the same department as Simon Little.
    - (D) She would like to change jobs.

Travel & Hotels 1

Part 5

Incomplete Sentences

Select the best answer to complete the sentence. Then choose the letter (A), (B), (C), or (D).

1. Sometimes it is ------- to travel by bullet train than by plane.

   (A) quick   (B) quickly   (C) fastest   (D) faster

2. The train will travel ------- some historical and cultural areas.

   (A) for   (B) forward   (C) through   (D) at

3. A passport allows ------- to travel to foreign countries.

   (A) every   (B) one   (C) your   (D) my

4. Your bags are checked through to Tokyo so you'll ------- them up at the airport there.

   (A) receive   (B) get   (C) pick   (D) take

5. We provide the ticket reservation system, with which a ticket can -------.

   (A) reserve   (B) was reserved   (C) reserved   (D) be reserved

6. A visit to Asakusa was not included in the ------- version of the itinerary.

   (A) all   (B) final   (C) decide   (D) finish

7. Take a moment to review the ------- instruction card in the seat pocket in front of you.

   (A) safe   (B) safety   (C) safely   (D) safer

8. The Wayfarer luggage set features five pieces that are ------- lightweight and durable.

   (A) both   (B) also   (C) neither   (D) whether

Text Completion

Select the best answer to complete the text. Then choose the letter (A), (B), (C), or (D).

Questions 9-12 refer to the following advertisement.

Star Travel is happy to ------ its new Star Passenger Points System. All hotels,
        9.

plane tickets, and car rentals booked through our website, startravel.com, will

result in rewards like discounts and upgrades on hotel stays, car rentals, you

name it! ------ to accumulate your points and, before you know it, you'll be
       10.

eligible for things like ------ hotel rooms and flights. ------.
                         11.   **12.**

9. (A) allow   (B) introduce   (C) teach   (D) say

10. (A) Choose   (B) Choosing   (C) Chose   (D) Chosen

11. (A) remote   (B) tentative   (C) initial   (D) complimentary

12. (A) Come into our store for more information.
    (B) Click here for a tour of our hotel.
    (C) We will contact you with an application form.
    (D) Check out our website for more details.

Reading Comprehension

Select the best answer for each question and mark the letter (A), (B), (C), or (D).

Questions 13-17 refer to the following e-mail and schedule.

From: katypirri@hawaiitourcompany.com
To: ktakemura@worldtourjapan.com
Date: December 5
Subject: Possible Schedule Changes

Dear Ms. Takemura,

I hope you are doing well. This e-mail is about the schedule for the February tour we are planning for your company. I have some issues I would like to discuss with you.

The company we use for the Hula Show is changing management. The new management is going to focus more on long-term hotel contracts and not short one-shot tour visits like ours. We have already found a replacement company, but I'm afraid it will increase the budget.

In addition, we have run into another problem with the Volcano Visit. The fees for National Park visits on weekends has increased. This was something we forgot to include when making the budget for your tour. This was clearly our mistake. I would like to ask if it would be OK to choose a new venue for our Farewell Dinner that will be cheaper. By doing so, the original budget will remain the same, even with a new Hula Show company.

Finally, I noticed that two water-based events have been scheduled in a row. It has been my experience that it may be better to schedule a non-beach day in between water days as guests may be dealing with body fatigue or sunburn and need time to recover. My suggestion is to move the 2nd water-based event to the following day, and, as the Cooking Class is near the Mall, move the 2nd shopping experience to that time.

Please let me know your thoughts on these suggestions.

Take care and I hope to hear from you soon,

Katy Pirri, Manager
Hawaii Tour Company

WTJ's Hawaiian 5-Day Tour
www.worldtourjapan.co.jp

Sunday	Monday	Tuesday	Wednesday	Thursday
Volcano Visit	Kayaking	Snorkeling	Hula Show	Hiking
Shopping	Museum	Cooking Class	Shopping	Farm Tour
				Farewell Dinner

13. Why was the e-mail sent?

(A) To inquire about participant numbers

(B) To introduce a new manager

(C) To explain possible schedule changes

(D) To sell tickets for a new tour plan

14. What does Ms. Pirri say about the Hula Show?

(A) They will cancel it.

(B) They will change companies.

(C) It will take place in a hotel.

(D) The cost will decrease.

15. What does Ms. Pirri indicate about the Volcano Visit?

(A) They should change it to another day.

(B) They will replace it with a visit to a National Park.

(C) The price to enter the area has increased.

(D) Ms. Takemura mistakenly chose a weekend to visit.

16. What does Ms. Pirri suggest doing about the Farewell Dinner?

(A) Move it to a different day

(B) Change the start time

(C) Allow guests to choose the location

(D) Reserve a cheaper restaurant

17. What day does Ms. Pirri suggest snorkeling take place?

(A) Sunday

(B) Monday

(C) Tuesday

(D) Wednesday

Office

Part 5

Incomplete Sentences

Select the best answer to complete the sentence. Then choose the letter (A), (B), (C), or (D).

1. Grace is always the ------- to arrive to the office because she lives so close.

   (A) early   (B) earlier   (C) earliest   (D) earliness

2. Some people in our department need to ------- the training session next month.

   (A) get along with   (B) take part in   (C) catch up with   (D) get on with

3. Occasionally, our manager ------- will post a message in our online SNS group.

   (A) himself   (B) he   (C) his   (D) him

4. The sales representatives should be very familiar ------- this software.

   (A) for   (B) on   (C) with   (D) in

5. The new high-speed Internet system has ------- in the office.

   (A) been installed   (B) installed   (C) been installing   (D) install

6. Employees working from home have become increasingly -------.

   (A) potential   (B) enable   (C) available   (D) common

7. The meeting was ------- scheduled for March 15.

   (A) initial   (B) initially   (C) initialize   (D) initializing

8. ------- I was reporting on our recent sales conference to Jessica, William came into the room with the bad news.

   (A) How   (B) When   (C) Because   (D) Only

Text Completion

Select the best answer to complete the text. Then choose the letter (A), (B), (C), or (D).

Questions 9-12 refer to the following web page.

Focuser is computer software that ------ businesses to improve office
9.
productivity and efficiency. Focuser restricts accessibility to social media,
shopping, videos, and games so staff have no distractions and effectively
spend their time ------ the work day. Companies can enjoy the flexibility the
10.
software provides. ------. Install the software on anything from office desktops,
11.
laptops, even mobile ------. Click here for more plans and payment-option
12.
information.

9. (A) allow   (B) allowing   (C) allowed   (D) allows

10. (A) while   (B) during   (C) when   (D) until

11. (A) We choose the software limits for your company.
     (B) Software limits are decided by management.
     (C) Use the special computers we provide you.
     (D) We will make your employees follow the rules.

12. (A) services   (B) instruments   (C) tools   (D) devices

Part 7

Reading Comprehension

Select the best answer for each question and mark the letter (A), (B), (C), or (D).

Questions 13-17 refer to the following web page and e-mails.

---

https://yourcomputerresource.com/picks/best-video-conferencing-software

The Best Video Conferencing Software for Today's Modern Workplace

For a company to stay healthy in these troublesome times, regular work-from-home arrangements are very important. We have tested and compared all the video conferencing software solutions to help you choose the right one to stay connected and ahead of the competition.

Here are our top picks:

Zoomba Meetings

This popular company offers simple video conferencing solutions but still has some problems with security. However, a free plan that offers so much value might be the best choice for some companies.

Anytime Video Meetings (AVM)

AVM has the most features of all the video software we checked. Because of this, it may be a little complicated for some people. There is a free version, and plans are available for very reasonable fees.

DoKoDemo Meeting

The most reliable and secure software is DoKoDemo Meeting. The features are basic, however the membership plans are a little expensive and there is no free version available. For the company looking for security and with a larger budget, this might be the best choice.

From: karencummings@jtbusinesssolutions.com
To: norikowagatsuma@jtbusinesssolutions.com
Date: March 22
Subject: video conferencing ideas

Hi Noriko,

I received the web page link you sent me. Thank you. I plan to tell employees about our new work-from-home policy at tomorrow's meeting. After I go over some of the details, I want to introduce the software we plan to use. I need to ask you to come to a decision about this and inform me soon. Head office is really pressing me to tell them what we plan to do. The vice-president, Jerry Miller, may come to our branch office tomorrow to sit in on the meeting. You may remember him from last year. He's someone I don't want to make angry.

I'm looking forward to hearing about your suggestion later today.

Karen Cummings
Branch Manager

From: norikowagatsuma@jtbusinesssolutions.com
To: karencummings@jtbusinesssolutions.com
Date: March 22
Subject: RE: video conferencing ideas

Good afternoon Karen,

Thank you for your e-mail. I have done a little more research and have some thoughts I should share with you now. As you know, one option, despite being popular, has some serious security issues. Many companies have a problem with this, and is something we also have to consider. AVM and DoKoDemo are both good options. One has a free version and one does not. I know we have a budget for this, so I think I am going to recommend that we spend the money to use something with the best security. I plan to talk about this possibility with the computer help desk people before coming by your office later today with a more detailed plan.

Please let me know what time I should come by.

Sincerely,

Noriko Wagatsuma

13. **What is the purpose of this web page?**

   (A) To advertise different computers

   (B) To give information on various options

   (C) To rank popular Internet companies

   (D) To promote its paid website membership

14. **What is inferred about Ms. Cummings?**

   (A) She used to work at head office.

   (B) She is new to the company.

   (C) Ms. Wagatsuma is her boss.

   (D) She is Ms. Wagatsuma's manager.

15. **What does Ms. Cummings ask Ms. Wagatsuma to do?**

   (A) Talk about the new work-from-home policy

   (B) Meet with Jerry Miller to discuss policy ideas

   (C) Suggest which product they should use

   (D) Inform employees at tomorrow's meeting

16. **According to the second e-mail, what is Ms. Wagatsuma's opinion?**

   (A) Zoomba would be good for the company.

   (B) AVM is too expensive to use.

   (C) DoKoDemo would be the best choice.

   (D) None of the options would be appropriate.

17. **What will Ms. Wagatsuma do next?**

   (A) Submit her proposal

   (B) Research more solutions

   (C) Discuss things with colleagues

   (D) Go to Ms. Cummings' office

Travel & Hotels 2

Incomplete Sentences

Select the best answer to complete the sentence. Then choose the letter (A), (B), (C), or (D).

1. Some airlines may not ------- last minute check-ins.

   (A) accept   (B) be accepted   (C) accepting   (D) to accept

2. Please note ------- advance that schedules are subject to change without prior notice.

   (A) for   (B) out   (C) in   (D) before

3. Mr. Yamada assists Ms. Hahn while ------- conducts a tour of European countries.

   (A) hers   (B) she   (C) herself   (D) her

4. If you use the public transportation, it is ------- getting a ticket that covers several days.

   (A) expensive   (B) worth   (C) fluent   (D) positive

5. This hotel proudly offers guests an unparalleled level of -------.

   (A) comforting   (B) comfortably   (C) comfortable   (D) comfort

6. All flights have ------- due to the bad weather.

   (A) been arrived   (B) been departed   (C) been delayed   (D) been booked

7. The bus ticket ------- to be purchased at a ticket center or travel agency.

   (A) has   (B) having   (C) have   (D) to have

8. Thank you for forwarding to us the ------- for our upcoming trip to Canada.

   (A) itinerary   (B) destination   (C) transportation   (D) reservation

Text Completion

Select the best answer to complete the text. Then choose the letter (A), (B), (C), or (D).

Questions 9-12 refer to the following letter.

November 21

Dear Michael Scott,

I am writing this letter because I am interested in the opening for the Tour Guide ------- your company, Sunshine Tours. This job opening came to my ------
9.   10.
through your job posting on your website.

My skills include knowledge of Southeast Asian history, fluency in three languages, and the ability to be a team player. After ------ your company, I feel
11.
my goals and values match those of Sunshine Tours.

Thank you for taking the time to review my resume. ------.
12.

Sincerely.

Ayana Tanaka

ENC: Resume

9. (A) by   (B) from   (C) with   (D) on

10. (A) interest   (B) mind   (C) attention   (D) eyes

11. (A) research   (B) researched   (C) researching (D) researches

12. (A) I look forward to hearing from you about a possible interview.
    (B) I can begin to work from the beginning of the new year.
    (C) I will call you to schedule an interview.
    (D) I would like to offer you the position as soon as possible.

Part 7

Reading Comprehension

Select the best answer for each question and mark the letter (A), (B), (C), or (D).

Questions 13-17 refer to the following web page and e-mails.

http//www.fairmonthotel.com/goldroom

The New Fairmont Hotel Gold Room

Our renovated Gold Rooms now have added comfort in a more beautiful environment. New features for all rooms include a home theatre with online streaming; marble bathrooms with walk-in shower; and a wide range of bath amenities, including Queen Life Soaps®.

Bed Size

One King, or one Queen bed, or two Double beds — depending on the room

Room View

Various cityscapes

Please note, photos are only representative. Actual rooms may vary.

Common Amenities

Private check-in/check-out on the 18th floor

Access to the Gold Lounge, offering complimentary breakfast and evening desserts

Complimentary Wi-Fi

Extra thick bath towels and robes

Refreshment center with coffee machine and kettle

Amenities upon Request *(fee required)*

Personal Bar Area (in some rooms) : fully stocked upon request.

City Concierge: help design your itinerary and access to the city's best experiences.

Special Occasion Amenity: birthdays, anniversaries, honeymoons, and special moments – we will do everything to make it a lifetime memory.

From: jeffwinger1972@queenlifesoap.com
To: reservations@fairmonthotel.com
Date: March 18
Subject: Gold Room Stay

To whom it may concern,

I recently had the pleasure of staying in one of your remodeled Gold Rooms. My soap company has the contract to provide you with amenities for these bathrooms. Thanks to our new work relationship, I was given the opportunity to stay in one of these rooms free of charge. Thank you again for this wonderful experience.

However, I do have a couple of concerns that I feel I should share with you. As I was staying by myself, I asked for a room with a single bed, but was surprised to see that my request was not met. I wonder how this mistake happened. Also, there was a small problem in that my free Wi-Fi was extremely slow. If I were a paying guest I might not be satisfied with this arrangement.

Other than that, I had a wonderful visit.

Thank you again,

Jeff Winger
Accounts Manager
Queen Life Soap Co.

From: reservations@fairmonthotel.com
To: jeffwinger1972@queenlifesoap.com
Date: March 19
Subject: Re: Gold Room Stay

Dear Mr. Winger,

Thank you for your valuable comments. We want to make this one of the best hotel experiences in the city, so if there are problems, we'd like to address them immediately.

You may be happy to know that Wi-Fi will be improved, not just for Gold Rooms, but for the entire hotel this weekend, as we'll be installing new Wi-Fi systems on all floors. Poor Wi-Fi will no longer be a problem at our hotel.

About your other concern, I'm in touch with the reservation office to see why you were given the room you stayed in. I suspect that it was the only room available, as paying guests will always get priority over non-paying guests. If there was another reason I am not aware of, I'll contact you with a brief e-mail explaining the decision by the reservation office.

Sincerely,

Jenn Tran
Hospitality Manager
Fairmont Hotel

13. According to the web page, what is an option for Gold Room guests?

(A) Home theater

(B) Wi-Fi access

(C) Use of Lounge

(D) Stocked bar

14. What is true about Gold Rooms?

(A) All requests are complimentary.

(B) Rooms may look different depending on the location.

(C) Guests can choose the view for their room.

(D) All rooms have the same bed type.

15. What is suggested about Mr. Winger's room?

(A) It had a king-sized bed.

(B) It had two double beds.

(C) It didn't have any soap.

(D) It didn't have Internet access.

16. What is true about Mr. Winger?

(A) He is a regular guest at the hotel.

(B) He helped renovate the hotel's rooms.

(C) His company supplies some of the amenities.

(D) His wife was unhappy with the hotel service.

17. What will Ms. Tran do for Mr. Winger?

(A) She will contact him when the Wi-Fi has improved.

(B) She will send him a hotel coupon.

(C) She will inform management about his complaints.

(D) She will notify him if she learns new information.

General

Incomplete Sentences

Select the best answer to complete the sentence. Then choose the letter (A), (B), (C), or (D).

1. Although Mr. Wexler is not an economist -------, he predicts that interest rates will fall.

   (A) he   (B) his   (C) him   (D) himself

2. Many experts wonder if this growth is -------.

   (A) considerable   (B) favorable   (C) sustainable   (D) durable

3. Patrick will speak about ------- issues on behalf of his organizations.

   (A) political   (B) politics   (C) politician   (D) politically

4. A person ------- has completed the training course shall be qualified to teach this course.

   (A) which   (B) who   (C) whose   (D) why

5. One of the main roles for government is to promote social -------.

   (A) diversify   (B) diverse   (C) diversity   (D) diversely

6. Participants are asked to sit ------- in their seats until all political commentators have exited.

   (A) quietly   (B) extremely   (C) exactly   (D) possibly

7. We need to ------- our manufacturing and labor costs.

   (A) reducing   (B) reduced   (C) reduce   (D) reduction

8. In compliance ------- the law, all passengers must undergo a customs inspection.

   (A) to   (B) out   (C) with   (D) along

Text Completion

Select the best answer to complete the text. Then choose the letter (A), (B), (C), or (D).

Questions 9-12 refer to the following article.

WINCHESTER (13 September) —— Winchester City council members have unanimously decided to pass a new hotel tax. From January, a 2% tax will be added to all hotel stays ------ city limits. The mayor said that money raised from
9.
the tax will be used for ------ Winchester's aging road system. The mayor added
10.
that without this new tax ------, maintaining the highways and roads in the city
11.
would be very difficult. ------. The main reason was that the hotels said it will
12.
make staying outside of city limits more attractive.

9. (A) at   (B) within   (C) over   (D) between

10. (A) improvement   (B) improve   (C) to improve   (D) improving

11. (A) revenue   (B) receipt   (C) stock   (D) salary

12. (A) If you oppose this decision, please write to the mayor.
    (B) Most of the roads in the city need immediate repair.
    (C) Hotels were united in opposition of the new tax.
    (D) Voting for the new mayor will happen next Monday.

Part 7

Reading Comprehension

Select the best answer for each question and mark the letter (A), (B), (C), or (D).

Questions 13-17 refer to the following e-mails and web page.

From: agarcia@geemail.com
To: inquiries@brightoncommunitycenter.com
Date: June 4
Subject: Summer Classes

To whom it may concern,

My name is Anna Garcia and I have some questions about the summer classes being offered at your community center. I read on the website that there are seven classes but according to the schedule it looks like it's eight weeks long. Is this a mistake? Also, I will be out of town the weekend of the August 1 for a family member's wedding and probably wouldn't make that Monday's class. Would I be able to makeup the missed class somehow?

Any information you could provide me would be appreciated.

Thank you,

Anna Garcia

---

http://www.brightoncommunitycenter.com

| Home | map | **course schedule** | Contact |

Brighton Community Center

7-Week course schedule Adults

Class	Fee	Time
Still Life Drawing	$60	Wednesdays, July 1 - August 26
Japanese for Beginners	$80	Mondays, July 6 - August 31
Kickboxing	$70	Fridays, July 3 - August 28
French for Beginners	$50	Thursdays, July 2 - August 27

· *Classes start at 7:00 P.M. and finish at 8:00 P.M.*
· *Application deadline is June 15 at 5:00 P.M. (No applications will be accepted after this time.)*
· *No refunds after the 2nd week of classes.*

*** Class canceled the week of July 20 due to Center renovations ***

62

From: inquiries@brightoncommunitycenter.com
To: agarcia@geemail.com
Date: June 5
Subject: Re: Summer Classes

Hello Ms. Garcia,

Thank you for inquiring about our popular summer classes. Let me mention that although the deadline for applications is next week, once a class is full, there will be no more students accepted, so please apply soon. You should know that the language classes are always the most popular.

You're correct about the number of classes and length of the schedule. It's not very clear on the web page as the information is at the very bottom, but we will not be open for a week towards the end of July.

Unfortunately, you cannot makeup for any missed classes. I suggest talking to the instructor about your situation and maybe he or she will make special arrangements with you to get that week's materials.

Sincerely,

Beth Osborne
Public Relations, Brighton Community Center
2251 Main Street, Brighton City

13. Why might Ms. Garcia miss one of the classes?

    (A) She'll be away on business.

    (B) She'll take a vacation overseas.

    (C) She'll be getting married.

    (D) She'll attend a relative's wedding.

14. What class is Ms. Garcia most likely interested in taking?

    (A) Still Life Drawing

    (B) Japanese for Beginners

    (C) Kickboxing

    (D) French for Beginners

15. According to the web page, what do students need to do?

    (A) Check the Center website for updates

    (B) Choose their classes after the 2nd week

    (C) Strictly observe the registration date and time

    (D) Pay the class fee in cash

16. What does Ms. Osborne say about the class schedule?

    (A) There will be a break due to venue closure.

    (B) There is a mistake on the web page.

    (C) It may change depending on student numbers.

    (D) Ms. Garcia is mistaken about the schedule.

17. What does Ms. Osborne suggest to Ms. Garcia?

    (A) Submit an official request for a makeup class

    (B) Talk to the teacher about her situation

    (C) Access the class materials from the web page

    (D) Take a different class on a different day

Scene 4

DATE ___ / ___ / ___

1. Ⓐ Ⓑ Ⓒ Ⓓ   9. Ⓐ Ⓑ Ⓒ Ⓓ
2. Ⓐ Ⓑ Ⓒ Ⓓ   10. Ⓐ Ⓑ Ⓒ Ⓓ
3. Ⓐ Ⓑ Ⓒ Ⓓ   11. Ⓐ Ⓑ Ⓒ Ⓓ
4. Ⓐ Ⓑ Ⓒ Ⓓ   12. Ⓐ Ⓑ Ⓒ Ⓓ
5. Ⓐ Ⓑ Ⓒ Ⓓ   13. Ⓐ Ⓑ Ⓒ Ⓓ
6. Ⓐ Ⓑ Ⓒ Ⓓ   14. Ⓐ Ⓑ Ⓒ Ⓓ
7. Ⓐ Ⓑ Ⓒ Ⓓ   15. Ⓐ Ⓑ Ⓒ Ⓓ
8. Ⓐ Ⓑ Ⓒ Ⓓ   16. Ⓐ Ⓑ Ⓒ Ⓓ

STUDENT ID _____

NAME _____

TODAY'S SCORE

Scene 1

DATE ___ / ___ / ___

1. Ⓐ Ⓑ Ⓒ Ⓓ   9. Ⓐ Ⓑ Ⓒ Ⓓ
2. Ⓐ Ⓑ Ⓒ Ⓓ   10. Ⓐ Ⓑ Ⓒ Ⓓ
3. Ⓐ Ⓑ Ⓒ Ⓓ   11. Ⓐ Ⓑ Ⓒ Ⓓ
4. Ⓐ Ⓑ Ⓒ Ⓓ   12. Ⓐ Ⓑ Ⓒ Ⓓ
5. Ⓐ Ⓑ Ⓒ Ⓓ   13. Ⓐ Ⓑ Ⓒ Ⓓ
6. Ⓐ Ⓑ Ⓒ Ⓓ   14. Ⓐ Ⓑ Ⓒ Ⓓ
7. Ⓐ Ⓑ Ⓒ Ⓓ   15. Ⓐ Ⓑ Ⓒ Ⓓ
8. Ⓐ Ⓑ Ⓒ Ⓓ   16. Ⓐ Ⓑ Ⓒ Ⓓ

STUDENT ID _____

NAME _____

TODAY'S SCORE

Scene 5

DATE ___ / ___ / ___

1. Ⓐ Ⓑ Ⓒ Ⓓ   9. Ⓐ Ⓑ Ⓒ Ⓓ
2. Ⓐ Ⓑ Ⓒ Ⓓ   10. Ⓐ Ⓑ Ⓒ Ⓓ
3. Ⓐ Ⓑ Ⓒ Ⓓ   11. Ⓐ Ⓑ Ⓒ Ⓓ
4. Ⓐ Ⓑ Ⓒ Ⓓ   12. Ⓐ Ⓑ Ⓒ Ⓓ
5. Ⓐ Ⓑ Ⓒ Ⓓ   13. Ⓐ Ⓑ Ⓒ Ⓓ
6. Ⓐ Ⓑ Ⓒ Ⓓ   14. Ⓐ Ⓑ Ⓒ Ⓓ
7. Ⓐ Ⓑ Ⓒ Ⓓ   15. Ⓐ Ⓑ Ⓒ Ⓓ
8. Ⓐ Ⓑ Ⓒ Ⓓ   16. Ⓐ Ⓑ Ⓒ Ⓓ

STUDENT ID _____

NAME _____

TODAY'S SCORE

Scene 2

DATE ___ / ___ / ___

1. Ⓐ Ⓑ Ⓒ Ⓓ   9. Ⓐ Ⓑ Ⓒ Ⓓ
2. Ⓐ Ⓑ Ⓒ Ⓓ   10. Ⓐ Ⓑ Ⓒ Ⓓ
3. Ⓐ Ⓑ Ⓒ Ⓓ   11. Ⓐ Ⓑ Ⓒ Ⓓ
4. Ⓐ Ⓑ Ⓒ Ⓓ   12. Ⓐ Ⓑ Ⓒ Ⓓ
5. Ⓐ Ⓑ Ⓒ Ⓓ   13. Ⓐ Ⓑ Ⓒ Ⓓ
6. Ⓐ Ⓑ Ⓒ Ⓓ   14. Ⓐ Ⓑ Ⓒ Ⓓ
7. Ⓐ Ⓑ Ⓒ Ⓓ   15. Ⓐ Ⓑ Ⓒ Ⓓ
8. Ⓐ Ⓑ Ⓒ Ⓓ   16. Ⓐ Ⓑ Ⓒ Ⓓ

STUDENT ID _____

NAME _____

TODAY'S SCORE

Scene 6

DATE ___ / ___ / ___

1. Ⓐ Ⓑ Ⓒ Ⓓ   9. Ⓐ Ⓑ Ⓒ Ⓓ
2. Ⓐ Ⓑ Ⓒ Ⓓ   10. Ⓐ Ⓑ Ⓒ Ⓓ
3. Ⓐ Ⓑ Ⓒ Ⓓ   11. Ⓐ Ⓑ Ⓒ Ⓓ
4. Ⓐ Ⓑ Ⓒ Ⓓ   12. Ⓐ Ⓑ Ⓒ Ⓓ
5. Ⓐ Ⓑ Ⓒ Ⓓ   13. Ⓐ Ⓑ Ⓒ Ⓓ
6. Ⓐ Ⓑ Ⓒ Ⓓ   14. Ⓐ Ⓑ Ⓒ Ⓓ
7. Ⓐ Ⓑ Ⓒ Ⓓ   15. Ⓐ Ⓑ Ⓒ Ⓓ
8. Ⓐ Ⓑ Ⓒ Ⓓ   16. Ⓐ Ⓑ Ⓒ Ⓓ

STUDENT ID _____

NAME _____

TODAY'S SCORE

Scene 3

DATE ___ / ___ / ___

1. Ⓐ Ⓑ Ⓒ Ⓓ   9. Ⓐ Ⓑ Ⓒ Ⓓ
2. Ⓐ Ⓑ Ⓒ Ⓓ   10. Ⓐ Ⓑ Ⓒ Ⓓ
3. Ⓐ Ⓑ Ⓒ Ⓓ   11. Ⓐ Ⓑ Ⓒ Ⓓ
4. Ⓐ Ⓑ Ⓒ Ⓓ   12. Ⓐ Ⓑ Ⓒ Ⓓ
5. Ⓐ Ⓑ Ⓒ Ⓓ   13. Ⓐ Ⓑ Ⓒ Ⓓ
6. Ⓐ Ⓑ Ⓒ Ⓓ   14. Ⓐ Ⓑ Ⓒ Ⓓ
7. Ⓐ Ⓑ Ⓒ Ⓓ   15. Ⓐ Ⓑ Ⓒ Ⓓ
8. Ⓐ Ⓑ Ⓒ Ⓓ   16. Ⓐ Ⓑ Ⓒ Ⓓ

STUDENT ID _____

NAME _____

TODAY'S SCORE

Scene 10

1. Ⓐ Ⓑ Ⓒ Ⓓ   9. Ⓐ Ⓑ Ⓒ Ⓓ
2. Ⓐ Ⓑ Ⓒ Ⓓ   10. Ⓐ Ⓑ Ⓒ Ⓓ
3. Ⓐ Ⓑ Ⓒ Ⓓ   11. Ⓐ Ⓑ Ⓒ Ⓓ
4. Ⓐ Ⓑ Ⓒ Ⓓ   12. Ⓐ Ⓑ Ⓒ Ⓓ
5. Ⓐ Ⓑ Ⓒ Ⓓ   13. Ⓐ Ⓑ Ⓒ Ⓓ
6. Ⓐ Ⓑ Ⓒ Ⓓ   14. Ⓐ Ⓑ Ⓒ Ⓓ
7. Ⓐ Ⓑ Ⓒ Ⓓ   15. Ⓐ Ⓑ Ⓒ Ⓓ
8. Ⓐ Ⓑ Ⓒ Ⓓ   16. Ⓐ Ⓑ Ⓒ Ⓓ

STUDENT ID

NAME

TODAY'S SCORE

Scene 7

1. Ⓐ Ⓑ Ⓒ Ⓓ   9. Ⓐ Ⓑ Ⓒ Ⓓ
2. Ⓐ Ⓑ Ⓒ Ⓓ   10. Ⓐ Ⓑ Ⓒ Ⓓ
3. Ⓐ Ⓑ Ⓒ Ⓓ   11. Ⓐ Ⓑ Ⓒ Ⓓ
4. Ⓐ Ⓑ Ⓒ Ⓓ   12. Ⓐ Ⓑ Ⓒ Ⓓ
5. Ⓐ Ⓑ Ⓒ Ⓓ   13. Ⓐ Ⓑ Ⓒ Ⓓ
6. Ⓐ Ⓑ Ⓒ Ⓓ   14. Ⓐ Ⓑ Ⓒ Ⓓ
7. Ⓐ Ⓑ Ⓒ Ⓓ   15. Ⓐ Ⓑ Ⓒ Ⓓ
8. Ⓐ Ⓑ Ⓒ Ⓓ   16. Ⓐ Ⓑ Ⓒ Ⓓ

STUDENT ID

NAME

TODAY'S SCORE

Scene 11

1. Ⓐ Ⓑ Ⓒ Ⓓ   9. Ⓐ Ⓑ Ⓒ Ⓓ
2. Ⓐ Ⓑ Ⓒ Ⓓ   10. Ⓐ Ⓑ Ⓒ Ⓓ
3. Ⓐ Ⓑ Ⓒ Ⓓ   11. Ⓐ Ⓑ Ⓒ Ⓓ
4. Ⓐ Ⓑ Ⓒ Ⓓ   12. Ⓐ Ⓑ Ⓒ Ⓓ
5. Ⓐ Ⓑ Ⓒ Ⓓ   13. Ⓐ Ⓑ Ⓒ Ⓓ
6. Ⓐ Ⓑ Ⓒ Ⓓ   14. Ⓐ Ⓑ Ⓒ Ⓓ
7. Ⓐ Ⓑ Ⓒ Ⓓ   15. Ⓐ Ⓑ Ⓒ Ⓓ
8. Ⓐ Ⓑ Ⓒ Ⓓ   16. Ⓐ Ⓑ Ⓒ Ⓓ
               17. Ⓐ Ⓑ Ⓒ Ⓓ

STUDENT ID

NAME

TODAY'S SCORE

Scene 8

1. Ⓐ Ⓑ Ⓒ Ⓓ   9. Ⓐ Ⓑ Ⓒ Ⓓ
2. Ⓐ Ⓑ Ⓒ Ⓓ   10. Ⓐ Ⓑ Ⓒ Ⓓ
3. Ⓐ Ⓑ Ⓒ Ⓓ   11. Ⓐ Ⓑ Ⓒ Ⓓ
4. Ⓐ Ⓑ Ⓒ Ⓓ   12. Ⓐ Ⓑ Ⓒ Ⓓ
5. Ⓐ Ⓑ Ⓒ Ⓓ   13. Ⓐ Ⓑ Ⓒ Ⓓ
6. Ⓐ Ⓑ Ⓒ Ⓓ   14. Ⓐ Ⓑ Ⓒ Ⓓ
7. Ⓐ Ⓑ Ⓒ Ⓓ   15. Ⓐ Ⓑ Ⓒ Ⓓ
8. Ⓐ Ⓑ Ⓒ Ⓓ   16. Ⓐ Ⓑ Ⓒ Ⓓ

STUDENT ID

NAME

TODAY'S SCORE

Scene 12

1. Ⓐ Ⓑ Ⓒ Ⓓ   9. Ⓐ Ⓑ Ⓒ Ⓓ
2. Ⓐ Ⓑ Ⓒ Ⓓ   10. Ⓐ Ⓑ Ⓒ Ⓓ
3. Ⓐ Ⓑ Ⓒ Ⓓ   11. Ⓐ Ⓑ Ⓒ Ⓓ
4. Ⓐ Ⓑ Ⓒ Ⓓ   12. Ⓐ Ⓑ Ⓒ Ⓓ
5. Ⓐ Ⓑ Ⓒ Ⓓ   13. Ⓐ Ⓑ Ⓒ Ⓓ
6. Ⓐ Ⓑ Ⓒ Ⓓ   14. Ⓐ Ⓑ Ⓒ Ⓓ
7. Ⓐ Ⓑ Ⓒ Ⓓ   15. Ⓐ Ⓑ Ⓒ Ⓓ
8. Ⓐ Ⓑ Ⓒ Ⓓ   16. Ⓐ Ⓑ Ⓒ Ⓓ
               17. Ⓐ Ⓑ Ⓒ Ⓓ

STUDENT ID

NAME

TODAY'S SCORE

Scene 9

1. Ⓐ Ⓑ Ⓒ Ⓓ   9. Ⓐ Ⓑ Ⓒ Ⓓ
2. Ⓐ Ⓑ Ⓒ Ⓓ   10. Ⓐ Ⓑ Ⓒ Ⓓ
3. Ⓐ Ⓑ Ⓒ Ⓓ   11. Ⓐ Ⓑ Ⓒ Ⓓ
4. Ⓐ Ⓑ Ⓒ Ⓓ   12. Ⓐ Ⓑ Ⓒ Ⓓ
5. Ⓐ Ⓑ Ⓒ Ⓓ   13. Ⓐ Ⓑ Ⓒ Ⓓ
6. Ⓐ Ⓑ Ⓒ Ⓓ   14. Ⓐ Ⓑ Ⓒ Ⓓ
7. Ⓐ Ⓑ Ⓒ Ⓓ   15. Ⓐ Ⓑ Ⓒ Ⓓ
8. Ⓐ Ⓑ Ⓒ Ⓓ   16. Ⓐ Ⓑ Ⓒ Ⓓ

STUDENT ID

NAME

TODAY'S SCORE

Scene 13

DATE   /   /

1. Ⓐ Ⓑ Ⓒ Ⓓ   9. Ⓐ Ⓑ Ⓒ Ⓓ
2. Ⓐ Ⓑ Ⓒ Ⓓ   10. Ⓐ Ⓑ Ⓒ Ⓓ
3. Ⓐ Ⓑ Ⓒ Ⓓ   11. Ⓐ Ⓑ Ⓒ Ⓓ
4. Ⓐ Ⓑ Ⓒ Ⓓ   12. Ⓐ Ⓑ Ⓒ Ⓓ
5. Ⓐ Ⓑ Ⓒ Ⓓ   13. Ⓐ Ⓑ Ⓒ Ⓓ
6. Ⓐ Ⓑ Ⓒ Ⓓ   14. Ⓐ Ⓑ Ⓒ Ⓓ
7. Ⓐ Ⓑ Ⓒ Ⓓ   15. Ⓐ Ⓑ Ⓒ Ⓓ
8. Ⓐ Ⓑ Ⓒ Ⓓ   16. Ⓐ Ⓑ Ⓒ Ⓓ
                17. Ⓐ Ⓑ Ⓒ Ⓓ

STUDENT ID

NAME

TODAY'S SCORE

Scene 14

DATE   /   /

1. Ⓐ Ⓑ Ⓒ Ⓓ   9. Ⓐ Ⓑ Ⓒ Ⓓ
2. Ⓐ Ⓑ Ⓒ Ⓓ   10. Ⓐ Ⓑ Ⓒ Ⓓ
3. Ⓐ Ⓑ Ⓒ Ⓓ   11. Ⓐ Ⓑ Ⓒ Ⓓ
4. Ⓐ Ⓑ Ⓒ Ⓓ   12. Ⓐ Ⓑ Ⓒ Ⓓ
5. Ⓐ Ⓑ Ⓒ Ⓓ   13. Ⓐ Ⓑ Ⓒ Ⓓ
6. Ⓐ Ⓑ Ⓒ Ⓓ   14. Ⓐ Ⓑ Ⓒ Ⓓ
7. Ⓐ Ⓑ Ⓒ Ⓓ   15. Ⓐ Ⓑ Ⓒ Ⓓ
8. Ⓐ Ⓑ Ⓒ Ⓓ   16. Ⓐ Ⓑ Ⓒ Ⓓ
                17. Ⓐ Ⓑ Ⓒ Ⓓ

STUDENT ID

NAME

TODAY'S SCORE

Scene 15

DATE   /   /

1. Ⓐ Ⓑ Ⓒ Ⓓ   9. Ⓐ Ⓑ Ⓒ Ⓓ
2. Ⓐ Ⓑ Ⓒ Ⓓ   10. Ⓐ Ⓑ Ⓒ Ⓓ
3. Ⓐ Ⓑ Ⓒ Ⓓ   11. Ⓐ Ⓑ Ⓒ Ⓓ
4. Ⓐ Ⓑ Ⓒ Ⓓ   12. Ⓐ Ⓑ Ⓒ Ⓓ
5. Ⓐ Ⓑ Ⓒ Ⓓ   13. Ⓐ Ⓑ Ⓒ Ⓓ
6. Ⓐ Ⓑ Ⓒ Ⓓ   14. Ⓐ Ⓑ Ⓒ Ⓓ
7. Ⓐ Ⓑ Ⓒ Ⓓ   15. Ⓐ Ⓑ Ⓒ Ⓓ
8. Ⓐ Ⓑ Ⓒ Ⓓ   16. Ⓐ Ⓑ Ⓒ Ⓓ
                17. Ⓐ Ⓑ Ⓒ Ⓓ

STUDENT ID

NAME

TODAY'S SCORE

PROFILE／著者略歴

Matthew Wilson（マシュー・ウィルソン）

宮城大学基盤教育群教授。
カナダ・トロント出身。カナダ、韓国、日本で長年、英語教育に携わる。仙台市教育委員会教育アドバイザーを経て2009年より宮城大学事業構想学部准教授、2016年より同教授、2017年より現職。研究分野は日本における英語教育と学生の動機づけ。米国のシェナンドア大学大学院卒業。同校より修士号取得（TESOL）。

鶴岡 公幸（つるおか ともゆき）

神田外語大学外国語学部教授。
神奈川県横浜市出身。キッコーマン（株）、（財）国際ビジネスコミュニケーション協会、KPMGあずさ監査法人、宮城大学食産業学部を経て、2014年より現職。1998年インディアナ大学経営大学院卒業。同校より経営学修士（MBA）取得。専門はマーケティング、ビジネス英語。TOEIC®関連書籍を含め著書、テキスト多数。

佐藤 千春（さとう ちはる）

株式会社and ENGLISH代表取締役。
山形県出身。岩手大学人文社会科学部卒業。山形県公立中学校英語教諭として14年間勤務。社会教育主事補資格取得。退職後、都内TOEIC®専門校講師兼マネージャーとしての勤務を経て、英語スクール『株式会社and ENGLISH』を起業。編集協力としてTOEIC®単語集の出版に携わる。

QUICK EXERCISES FOR THE TOEIC® L&R TEST 400 Reading
切り取り提出式 スコア別 TOEIC® L&R徹底対策ドリル400 リーディング編

2021年4月5日　初版第1刷発行

著　　者　Matthew Wilson／鶴岡公幸／佐藤千春

発 行 者　森　信久
発 行 所　**株式会社　松柏社**
　　　　　〒102-0072　東京都千代田区飯田橋1-6-1
　　　　　TEL　03（3230）4813（代表）
　　　　　FAX　03（3230）4857
　　　　　http://www.shohakusha.com
　　　　　e-mail: info@shohakusha.com

装　　幀　小島トシノブ（NONdesign）
本文レイアウト　　赤木健太郎（有限会社ケークルーデザインワークス）
組版・印刷・製本　シナノ書籍印刷株式会社
ISBN978-4-88198-764-3
略号＝764

Copyright © 2021 by Matthew Wilson, Tomoyuki Tsuruoka and Chiharu Sato